A Father's Guide To A Joyful,
Successful and Significant Life

A Father's Guide To A Joyful, Successful and Significant Life

"It's Simple – Just Not Easy"

Bob Campana

Copyright © 2015 by Bob Campana.

Library of Congress Control Number:	2015920124
ISBN: Hardcover	978-1-5144-3220-4
Softcover	978-1-5144-3219-8
eBook	978-1-5144-3218-1

All rights reserved. No part of this book may be reproduced or transmitted in any form or by any means, electronic or mechanical, including photocopying, recording, or by any information storage and retrieval system, without permission in writing from the copyright owner.

Scripture texts, prefaces, introductions, footnotes and cross references used in this work are taken from the New American Bible, revised edition © 2010, 1991, 1986, 1970 Confraternity of Christian Doctrine, Inc., Washington, DC All Rights Reserved.

Any people depicted in stock imagery provided by Thinkstock are models, and such images are being used for illustrative purposes only.
Certain stock imagery © Thinkstock.

Print information available on the last page.

Rev. date: 02/16/2021

To order additional copies of this book, contact:
Xlibris
844-714-8691
www.Xlibris.com
Orders@Xlibris.com
730087

December 2020

SIGNIFICANT EVENTS SINCE THE ORIGINAL PUBLICATION DATE 2015:

- All three of our children were married:
    - Anthony July 2, 2016
    - Lauren May 6, 2017
    - Nicole July 6, 2019

- Four beautiful and healthy granddaughters were born:
    - Sophia Grace December 19, 2017
    - Livia Carmen March 9, 2018 (My 59th birthday)
    - Ella Bove December 17, 2019
    - Demi Lincoln April 7, 2020

- I was diagnosed with HPV Positive Throat Cancer in 2017 and successfully defeated it. Thank you to Lee Koury, Dr. Ted Teknos and my awesome wife Lori.

- With my two year follow up from throat cancer, in 2020, a PET scan detected a nonsmoking lung cancer. This cancer was also successfully defeated with the help of Dr. Ted Teknos, Dr. Phil Linden (surgeon) and my awesome wife Lori. Below is a note I wrote, while I was in the hospital after my lung surgery.

Go Forward Plan – RMC

"I am blessed in countless ways. I will stand on gratitude and walk the talk of the servant leader that I am. My faith, family, health, freedom and integrity will guide my path. My time will be focused on my prioritized values. I will be an example to my family and friends – positive, joyful and selfless. Lori and I will celebrate 75 years of marriage healthy and joyful. She is the greatest blessing along with salvation. I will continue to honor God, Jesus and the Holy Spirit in a way that our children and future generations will see as the way to salvation and eternal life.

My cancer experience (throat and lung) will not define me. God will use my testimony to reach countless people to accept Jesus as Lord and Savior. God has a plan for me, and I will do my best to deliver. These lemons will be turned in lemonade. I welcome the opportunity to serve my Lord and Savior Jesus.

I love my wife, children and grandchildren beyond words. I will be an example for them to live a joyful, successful and significant life. Life is not easy, but it is a blessing. It is not without challenge, so the response is the key. We control very little – one is attitude, another is our integrity. God bless me, Lori and our family with good health and the fruits of the Holy Spirit."

- Lori and I traveled to many places. Since 2015, of particular note: Fatima and Lordes, to honor Mother Mary in 2018. We also traveled to the Holy Land to Honor God the Father, Son and Holy Ghost in 2018. Lake Como and a Rhine River Cruise from Switzerland to the Netherlands in 2017. A Danube River Cruise in 2019, including Germany, Austria, Budapest and Prague.

- Donald Trump was elected President.

- Covid 19 impacted the world in 2020.

PURPOSE

I stand on the shoulders of many wonderful people who came before me. At the age of 61, I am compelled to chronicle wisdom I have been abundantly blessed to obtain and share it with my family and future generations (an heirloom). My purpose is to inspire you to achieve more than you dreamed by learning as soon as possible simple proven secrets to a joyful, successful and significant life.

Simple is a word that truly inspires me. Leonoardo DaVinci says it best, "simplicity is the ultimate sophistication". Many people confuse simple for easy. Simple means not complicated. What I am offering is simple, just not easy. If you apply simple proven wisdom with discipline and hard work you can achieve and exceed your dreams. This guide is intentionally brief so you will be required to investigate topics more thoroughly on your own. It is designed as a guide to be lived by and referenced on an ongoing basis. Feel free to enhance this body of work and pass it along to our future generations.

My prayers and dreams are for each and every one of you to become great fathers or mothers and great servant leaders.

Jesus instructs us with the Ten Commandments of which they can be further reduced to two main commandments. Number one, love God with all your heart. Number two, love your neighbor. If you can focus on these two, simple, yet not easy commandments, I am certain you will have the foundation to learn and grow from so that you can live a joyful, successful and significant life. I pray that you accept Jesus as your Lord and savior and we all unite again in heaven.

MISSION STATEMENT

I believe you should be clear about my mindset as you drink from this fountain of wisdom I have assembled for you. I believe the simplest way to do that is by sharing my 2021 mission statement.

BOB CAMPANA'S 2021 MISSION STATEMENT

- I am obedient to God the Father, Son and Holy Spirit. I reap my God given talents. I gratefully, humbly, enthusiastically and with a strong sense of discipline welcome each day living by my prioritized values of faith, family, health, freedom and integrity.
- I am a dedicated, loyal, loving, supportive and fun husband, father, grandfather (papa), partner and friend. I take an interest in their individual interests and wellbeing. I demonstrate that "I care".
- I am life-long learner and continuous improver.
- I am a servant leader (selfless), mentor, example and role model for others.
- I live each day with a mindset of GHEDMCL: Grateful, Humble, Enthusiastic, Disciplined, Meek, Coachable and Great Listener.

DAILY PRAYER

Lord, please bless me and my family with good health, happiness and peace. Make us always cognizant of those less fortunate. Bless us with the Holy Spirit and the fruits of the Holy Spirit (Love, Joy, Peace, Patience, Kindness, Goodness, Gentleness and Self Control). Bless us with gratitude, humility, enthusiasm and discipline. When we are in positions of strength, bless us with meekness, always be coachable and allow us to be great listeners (GHEDMCL). Please forgive us for what we have said and not said, for what we have done and not done, for what we have thought and not thought. We are all sinners in need of you as our Savior. Thank you for my wonderful life, my wonderful wife and our wonderful family.

TOOLKIT FOR LIFE

I have long dreamed of somehow assembling proven tools into a simple format to benefit others. I have decided upon the "Toolkit For Life" made for those who strive to maximize their potential. I strongly encourage you to become "master craftsmen" of these ten simple, yet profoundly effective tools so you can live a joyful, successful and significant life.

TOOLS

1. The Bible
2. Mission Statement
3. Prioritized Values/Written Goals
4. Mindset
5. Exceed Expectations/Add Value
6. Lifelong Learning and Self-Improvement
7. The Golden Rule
8. Give It To Get It – The Law of Reciprocity
9. Handwritten Notes Of Appreciation
10. The Who In Your Life

Note:

1. You will be required to continuously monitor your level of competence for each tool. If you strive for perfection, you are sure to achieve excellence.
2. <u>This guide and this Toolkit for Life are meant to be lived not read one time and put on a shelf. It is a manual for life to be referenced continuously. Keep it near you and measure your progress.</u>

TOOLKIT FOR LIFE

TOOLKIT FOR LIFE
TOOL #1- THE BIBLE

The Bible is the most valuable resource the world will ever know. I am convinced the answers to all of life's questions are available to you in the Bible. I <u>regret not</u> embracing the Bible sooner in my life.

I want to share some simple facts about this awesome book:

- Sixty-six books make up the Bible
- Thirty-nine books in the Old Testament – before Jesus
- Twenty-seven books in the New Testament – after Jesus
- Written over 1,600 years ago by forty-four authors
- No other religion has multiple authors except Christianity

- No other religion has hundreds of prophecies (definition: the for- telling of what is to come) validating the truth.
- Jesus came to save us from sin, as we are all sinners. He offers the greatest gift ever known to man – salvation. (Definition: from the power and penalty of sin – eternal in heaven.)
- The Books of Proverbs, Ecclesiastes and Psalms are a treasure chest of wisdom.
- Embrace the Bible! Cherish it! Share it! Rely on it!

TOOLKIT FOR LIFE
TOOL #2 – MISSION STATEMENT

Who are you? Who do you want to become? Take the time to quietly draft your mission statement outlining your inner constitution. It will change over time, but the process of thought and the process of committing it to paper will help clarify your self-imposed expectations for conduct in life. This simple process will create a solid foundation from which you can seek your dreams in life. Be sure to share it with those close to you and be open and honest to feedback. Make the decision of who you are and who you want to become and live accordingly.

TOOLKIT FOR LIFE
TOOL #3 – PRIORITIZED VALUES/WRITTEN GOALS

Deciding what you value <u>most</u> in life will provide clarity and focus. All of us value many things. The problem becomes, what do you focus on? If you prioritize your values and work diligently to have them where you want them to be, you will be free to enjoy your less prioritized values without disrupting what is most important to you.

My prioritized values are:

1. Faith
2. Family
3. Health
4. Freedom – Personal and Financial
5. Integrity
6. Travel

Once you have determined your prioritized values (know they will change throughout your life), you can begin to effectively draft your written goals. Starting with the number one prioritized value, you can establish your dreams and expectations for your future. There are many sources and methods to learn how to draft your goals, so explore. I have included my 2021 written goals at the end of this guide for your reference. Know that my approach is unique to me, as your approach will be unique to you. There is no wrong way to do it – "Just Do It"!!!

Every year between Thanksgiving and New Years, I find a quiet place with pen and paper and dream about the upcoming year and the future. I utilize my previous year goals to reflect and move forward.

Written goals based upon prioritized values will dramatically enhance your life. Be sure to share them with your loved ones. Each year I share mine with Lori, Anthony, Lauren and Nicole. This insures they know what is most important to me as I move forward in life.

TOOLKIT FOR LIFE
TOOL #4 – MINDSET

You must make a decision to be responsible for yourself in all matters. Life is not fair, but it certainly is a gift from God so Carpe Diem (seize the day). Understand that Emotional Intelligence (EI) is much more important than IQ.

I firmly believe you must make a decision every day to have a mindset of GHEDMCL:

- **Grateful**: The mother of all virtues. An attitude of gratitude will make every day a great day. Today is a great day to make it a great day.
- **Humble**: There are two kinds of people in this world, those who are humble and those who are soon to be. Arrogance will be met with justice so be mindful of your

posture. Pride repels and humility attracts so decide upon humility and life will deliver accordingly.

- **Enthusiastic**: Enthusiasm is a priceless energy to enjoy and to share with others. I have added greatly to my personal and professional life by sharing my enthusiasm for life. I believe it to be an outpouring of my sincere gratitude for the blessings God grants me.
- **Disciplined**: I believe discipline is the glue that holds your dreams and goals together. Discipline and hard work are the great difference makers in life. You will either experience the pain of discipline or the pain of regret – know that the pain of regret far outweighs the pain of discipline. Chose discipline!
- **Meek**: Power under control. Often meekness is confused with weakness – nothing could be further from the truth. Never abuse your power. Be confident yet considerate.
- **Coachable**: Seek advice with enthusiasm! The power of guidance and wisdom from others has made a profound improvement on my life. I am certain it will do the same

for you. Let your coach/mentor know how much you appreciate their guidance and wisdom and you will be sure to continue to benefit from them. Do not let your pride intercept your great opportunity to learn from others.
- **Great Listener:** Very few people possess the skill of a great listener. Take an interest in others and you will witness magic in your life.

People want:

- To be listened to
- To Feel they matter
- To have meaning

People are looking for people who are:

- Trustworthy
- Kind
- Loyal
- Courageous
- Principled
- Competent
- Understanding
- Forgiving
- Selfless

So be that person.

Make the decision today to be grateful, humble, enthusiastic, disciplined, meek, coachable and a great listener. Emotional Intelligence (EI) will allow you to enjoy the fruits of life in countless ways.

TOOLKIT FOR LIFE
TOOL #5- EXCEED EXPECTATIONS AND ADD VALUE

Understanding what is expected of you is vital. Meeting expectations will get you through life in an acceptable manner. Exceeding expectations on a daily basis will propel you to heights you can only dream of. Thankfully I learned early in my life that when I exceeded expectations, opportunities presented themselves and my life was greatly enhanced by it. Ask yourself, how can I exceed the expectations of this situation? How can I add value to this situation? It could be your parent, friend, loved one, boss, teacher, coworker, partner, client, child etc. Give it a try and experience the benefits. Under Promise and Over Deliver. The fruits reaped will be exponential to your efforts sewn.

TOOLKIT FOR LIFE
TOOL #6 – LIFE-LONG LEARNING AND SELF-IMPROVEMENT

Not all readers are leaders, but all leaders are readers, so prioritize your time for reading. Your academic education is only the start. Take responsibility for yourself and invest in life long learning and self-improvement. I made a decision after I graduated from college to become a life long learner. I have found the daily pursuit of wisdom and self-improvement is not only enjoyable, but it is most beneficial to my personal and professional life. I take great pride in my libraries – at home and at my office. Start your library today! Books, people, experiences, lectures, travel, museums etc. - all provide unique opportunities to grow. I have found history and biographies to be of great value as well as cutting edge breakthroughs. Stoicism (the ancient Greek school of philosophy) is a subject to master. The four virtues of wisdom, justice, courage and moderation will serve you well. Drink often and deeply from the many fountains of wisdom for your entire life and teach future generations to do the same.

TOOLKIT FOR LIFE
TOOL #7 – THE GOLDEN RULE

Do unto others as you would have them do unto you is from the Bible – Matthew 7:12. I can tell you from experience that the fruit reaped is real and unlimited. As you build goodwill with others throughout your life, you literally build an account from which you will draw goodwill. I continue to be amazed by the many blessings showered upon my family, and me as I build my goodwill account through my daily use of the golden rule. Ask yourself how would you want the other person to treat you if they were in the reversed role then treat them accordingly. You will be amazed just by doing to/for others what you would want done to/for you will yield.

Note: The Golden Rule is one of the Dale Carnegie programs fundamental rules. I am a graduate of the course, as is Lori, Anthony, Lauren and Nicole. It is my dream that all future generations will join us as graduates. I consider the course a priceless contribution to my knowledge base.

TOOLKIT FOR LIFE
TOOL #8 – GIVE IT TO GET IT – LAW OF RECIPROCITY

The Bible refers to it as sowing and reaping. Whatever you want in life, give it and you will get it. If you want friends, be a friend. If you want respect, give respect. If you want love, give love. If you want compassion, give compassion. If you want money, give money. If you want success, you need to help others achieve success. As soon as you give away what you ultimately want, you will get what you want. Zig Ziglar says it the best, "you can get whatever you want in life if you help enough other people get what they want". Sow the seeds and reap the harvest.

TOOLKIT FOR LIFE
TOOL #9 – HANDWRITTEN NOTES OF APPRECIATION

The power of a sincere handwritten, hand-addressed note is beyond explanation. A sincere expression of your heart in writing will yield an incredible mutual satisfaction for you and the recipient. I have utilized this strategy for thirty plus years and never intend to stop. My annual goal is one hundred plus notes of love, gratitude, appreciation, congratulations and encouragement. I look for reasons to send them to those I care about. You may say one hundred plus notes per year is too many, and I say it is only two per week. I make a copy of each and put it in my "annual notes of appreciation" file. I review my file at year-end prior to my year-end notes to family and friends. You will set yourself apart and you will find great joy doing so. Begin today! Start with your mother, father and grandparents if you are fortunate enough to still have the opportunity to do so. Make a list and touch the people who matter most with a sincere expression of your heart in writing.

TOOLKIT FOR LIFE
TOOL #10 – THE WHO IN YOUR LIFE

The Who in Your Life will greatly influence your quality of life. You have great control over who you allow to impact your life - so chose wisely. Who you marry is the most important decision of all. Make sure your values are aligned, or you will be heading into a disaster - chose wisely!

Who you surround yourself with socially and professionally are a reflection on you in a dramatic fashion – chose wisely!

Who you seek counsel from is critical as you can benefit exponentially from great advisors and mentors. I have been blessed with many great mentors throughout my life starting with my mother and my father. Once I discovered how eager others are to help, I became a professional at seeking advice/assistance from people I admired and respected. The wisdom available is beyond explanation and it is free of charge. If you have a mindset to always assist others (servant leader), you will have a clear conscious to ask for advice/assistance yourself. Seek mentors actively and once you connect be sure to nourish the relationship. Show them respect, appreciation and admiration for their time and talents. I pay it forward my mentoring many young people. I enjoy the process and it allows me to pass along the wisdom I have been so abundantly blessed to receive. The Who in your life is your decision – Chose wisely!

Daily, Weekly, Monthly, Quarterly, Annually

It takes discipline to do what you know is best, but the rewards are priceless. I am certain you will find great value in the following:

- *Daily*: Pray, thank God for your countless blessings, read from the Bible, make your bed, brush your teeth (twice a day), floss, read to learn and improve, exercise, eat healthy (Whole Foods Plant Based), exceed expectations, add value, serve someone and smile. Have a mindset to be grateful, humble, enthusiastic, disciplined, meek, coachable and a great listener.
- *Weekly*: Worship God, send hand written notes, prepare for the next week.
- *Monthly*: Read a book (maybe 2, 3, or 4), review your goals and adjust your goals accordingly.

- *Quarterly*: Travel and review your financials.
- *Annually*: Review mission statement, prioritized values, rewrite goals, send year-end notes of appreciation, add to your gratitude journal, vote in every election and buy good shoes.
- *Biennially* – Travel the world and experience new cultures.
- *Note*: Diet has become paramount in our lives. Whole Foods Plant Based is best for you and your family. I am convinced oil is damaging to your vascular system and to be avoided when possible.

RECOMMENDED BOOKS

- The Bible - God
- Book of Proverbs (In the Bible – King Solomon)
- How To Win Friends and Influence People – Dale Carnegie
- The Last Lecture – Randy Pauch
- True Measure of a Man – Richard E. Simmons III
- The Wisdom of Wooden – Coach John Wooden
- Think and Grow Rich – Napoleon Hill
- Make Your Bed – Admiral William H. McRaven

- Treasury of Quotes – Jim Rohn
- Poor Charlie's Almanack – The Wit and Wisdom of Charles T. Munger – Peter D. Kaufman
- Prevent and Reverse Heart Disease – Dr. Caldwell B. Esselstyn Jr.

RECOMMENDED PUBLICATIONS

- 3-2-1 Thursday – James Clear
- Daily Stoics
- Gus Lloyd's – 60 Second Reflections
- Rich Roll Podcast
- Joe Rogan Podcast
- The Knowledge Project Podcast – Shane Parrish

AUTHORS

- Coach John Wooden
- Pastor Dick Woodward
- Billy Graham
- David McCullough
- Stephen Ambrose
- Pat Williams
- Dr. Kevin Elko
- Jim Rohn

- Zig Ziglar
- Napoleon Hill
- Steven R. Covey

BIOGRAPHIES

- Ben Franklin
- Abraham Lincoln
- George Washington
- Winston Churchill
- General George C. Marshall
- Abigail Adams
- Frances Hesselbein
- Thomas Jefferson
- Teddy Roosevelt
- Napoleon

QUOTES

- "We must all suffer from one of two pains. The pain of discipline or the pain of regret. The pain of regret far outweighs the pain of discipline. Chose Discipline." Jim Rohn
- "Nothing works unless you do." Maya Angelo

- "There is nothing anyone can do for an undisciplined person to make them successful." John Maxwell.
- "You do not rise in the level of your goals. You fall to the level of your systems. Your goal is your desired outcome. Your system is the collection of daily habits that will get you there. This year, spend less time focusing on outcomes and more time focusing on habits that preceed the results." James Clear
- "Constant honesty yields instant credibility." Leo Koury
- "Don't be a big hog, be a little pig. Big hogs get slaughtered and little pigs keep on eating." Patsie C. Campana Sr.
- "An investment in knowledge pays the best interest". Ben Franklin
- "You can't take your money to heaven but you can take your family". Coach Lou Holtz
- "Character cannot be developed in ease and quiet. Only through experience of trial and suffering can the soul be strengthened, ambition inspired and success achieved". Helen Keller

- "Courage doesn't always roar. Sometimes courage is a quiet voice at the end of the day saying, 'I'll try again tomorrow.'" Mary Anne Radmacher – favorite of my mother Jenee'
- "Only a life living for others is a life worthwhile". Albert Einstein
- "8th wonder of the world is dogged daily, incremental progress." Charlie Munger
- "People do not decide their futures, they decide their habits and their habits decide their futures". F. M. Alexander
- "You can get whatever you want in life if you help enough other people get what they want". Zig Ziglar
- "Ascending levels of intelligence: 5. Smart 4. Intelligent 3. Brilliant 2. Genius 1. Simple." Albert Einstein
- "Spread the sunshine". Bob Campana

RANDOM WORDS OF WISDOM

- The greatest thing a father can do for his children is to love their mother (and I do).
- Contentment can only be found in Jesus
- True strength is found in humility – kind and gentle, yet brave and strong.

- Arrogance will be met with justice.
- Living doesn't cost much but showing off does.
- There is never a right time to do the wrong thing and never a wrong time to do the right thing.
- When making plans, think big. When making progress think small.
- The power of the tongue can breathe life or death into a person – breathe life.
- Pride repels, humility attracts.
- Leadership is a privilege.
- Become a great listener - it's a powerful attribute.
- If not me, who? If not now, when? Just do it!
- Four days of climbing is wiped out by one day of coasting. Don't coast.
- There are some things you can't learn from others. You have to pass through the fire.
- Be a person of character and surround yourself with people of character.
- How to be happy:
    - Get outside every day.
    - Move: walk, exercise or dance.
    - Spend less than you earn.
    - View life as a play.

- Be the one who looks for solutions.
- Develop a bias to contribute and create.
- Learn from the lucky and successful.
- Be the first to say hello.
- Be reliable.
- Smile.

BIBLE VERSES

- 1 Corinthians 13:13 – So now faith, hope and love abide, these three; but the greatest of these is love.
- Galatians 5:22-23 – In contrast, the fruit of the Spirit is love, joy, peace, patience, kindness, goodness, faithfulness, gentleness, self-control; against such things there is no law.
- Galatians 6:7 – Make no mistake: God is not mocked, for a person will reap only what he sows,
- John 3:16 – For God so loved the world that he gave his only Son, so that everyone who believes in him might not perish but might have eternal life.
- John 10:10 – A thief comes only to steal and slaughter and destroy; I came so that

they might have life and have it more abundantly.
- John 15:5-8 – I am the vine, you are the branches. Whoever remains in me and I in him will bear much fruit, because without me you can do nothing. Anyone who does not remain in me will be thrown out like a branch and wither; people will gather them and throw them into a fire and they will be burned. If you remain in me and my words remain in you, ask for whatever you want and it ill be done for you. By this is my Father glorified, that you bear much fruit and become my disciples.
- Luke 11:9 – And I tell you, ask and you will receive; seek and you will find; knock and the door will be opened to you.
- Philippians 4:8 – Finally, brothers, whatever is true, whatever is honorable, whatever is just, whatever is pure, whatever is lovely, whatever is gracious, if there is any excellence and if there is anything worthy of praise, think about these things.
- Proverbs 15:22 - Plans fail when there is no counsel, but they succeed when advisers are many.

- Proverbs 18:21 – Death and life are in the power of the tongue; those who choose one shall eat its fruit.
- Proverbs 31:10 – An excellent wife who can find? She is far more precious than jewels.

CLOSING

Nobody cares how much you know, until they know how much you care. This guide is my way of demonstrating how much I care about you, my future generations so you will care about what I have come to know. I am certain this guide will significantly improve your life and your future. Drink deeply and repeatedly from this fountain of wisdom that I have assembled for your benefit and the benefit of our future generations. Please share this guide with your children, grandchildren and those you care about. Feel free to enhance it with additional wisdom moving forward and pass it along.

In closing, it is my dream for my family and future generations to experience a joyful, successful and significant life. Know your prioritized values. Pursue your dreams and goals with passion and discipline. Be proud of your family heritage of hard work, gratitude, humility, charity and kindness. Invest in your children and grandchildren so they may learn sooner rather than later how to navigate this tremendous blessing called life. When it is all over here on earth, I will be waiting for you in heaven. Be good, be kind, be considerate of the feelings of others and know I love you dearly.

Dad

SUPPLEMENTS

- Ten Secrets To Success
- 2021 Goals and Prioritized Values

10 SECRETS TO SUCCESS

I have been reading Investor's Business Daily for over 30 years. Each day on page 3 is "Leaders and Success". Great quotes and success articles have shaped me in a meaningful way. The 10 Secrets to Success are listed daily and I have found it to be the simplest, most impactful list of traits that when combined can turn dreams into reality. I have handed out hundreds of copies of the 10 Secrets to Success to those who demonstrated a willingness to reach for their dreams. I strongly suggest you subscribe to the publication and obtain a copy of the 10 Secrets To Success, www.investors.com. Carry a copy everyday to hand out to others once you have memorized them and begin to live by them as I do. "Carpe diem"

P.C. CAMPANA, INC.
1374 EAST 28th STREET
LORAIN, OHIO 44055

Values/Goals/Future

(440) 246-6500
(800) 321-0151
Fax: (440) 244-2693

12·29·20

PATSIE C. CAMPANA, SR.
FOUNDER

Wow, what a year 2020 turned out to be. Nobody could have predicted the world being turned upside down by COVID-19. The impact was felt by every family, every business and every organization. It validated for me we only control how we react to circumstances as almost everything is out of our control. We do control our mindset. I choose to be better not bitter. I choose to live in vision not circumstance. I choose to fight not give up. I choose to be a blessing not mean. I choose to forgive not condemn. I choose to be grateful not ungrateful. I choose to be humble not arrogant. I choose to be enthusiastic not low energy. I choose to be disciplined not undisciplined. I choose to be meek not ruthless. I choose to be coachable not all knowing. I choose to be a great listener not the center of attention. There is a big difference between choosing and feeling. Choose to win on 3 levels - Spiritual, Physical & Relational. Choose life not death, choose faith not fear. I want my family and future generations to choose to be great.

I am so grateful for so many things - Salvation, Lori, our family, our friends, our health, our freedoms, our opportunities. I am grateful for my parents, my mentors, my role models, my experiences, my business partners, my fellow board members, my career and my future. Knowing my family has accepted Jesus as Lord and Savior so we will be together for eternity.

Gratitude is my foundation and my fuel. It drives me to be my best and teach others to be their best. I am committed to be a selfless servant leader to my family, friends and others who demonstrate a desire help others.

2020 was pivotal in many ways. We welcomed Demi Lincoln to our family. Now we enjoy Sophia Grace, Livia Carmen, Ella Bove and Demi Lincoln as God's gifts to our family. I was diagnosed with non smoking lung cancer and by the grace of God caught it early and had it successfully removed in May. My commitment to health and wellness went to the highest level thanks to Lori (my angel). I am 100% whole food, plant based diet. Oil is my enemy and avoided when possible. I feel fantastic and look forward to celebrating our 75th wedding anniversary 6·4·58.

1 of 2

P.C. CAMPANA, INC.
1374 EAST 28th STREET
LORAIN, OHIO 44055

VALUES / GOALS / FUTURE

(440) 246-6500
(800) 321-0151
Fax: (440) 244-2693

12·29·20

PATSIE C. CAMPANA, SR.
FOUNDER

JAN +
WE TRAVELED TO UTAH FOR SKIING IN FEBRUARY. ENJOYED NAPLES IN MARCH. THEN THE LOCKDOWN STARTED AND CONTINUES FROM COVID-19. WE CAREFULLY TRAVELED TO
+ GREENBRIER, W.VA IN AUGUST
NAPLES AGAIN IN SEPTEMBER AND NOVEMBER. OUR TRAVEL PLANS FOR A RIVER CRUISE WITH MOE AND LENA RUGGIERO ON THE DANUBE RIVER WERE POSTPONED. WE PLANNED A TRIP OUT WEST FOR LATE SUMMER 2021 WITH OUR CRUISE GROUP. ONE WAY OR ANOTHER LORI AND I WILL MAKE THE BEST OF OUR CIRCUMSTANCES AND HAVE A LOT OF FUN. WE LOVE EACH OTHER SO MUCH AND ENJOY BEING TOGETHER ANYWHERE/ANYTIME.

2020 WAS AN AMAZING YEAR FOR OUR BUSINESS. WE SUCCESSFULLY COMPLETED THE PRESERVE AT QUARRY LAKES. WE ARE ENJOYING EXCEPTIONAL SUCCESS AT THE RESERVE AT BEAVER CREEK AND WE PLAN TO BREAK GROUND ON EAGLE RIDGE IN EARLY 2021. WE SECURED A 20 YEAR TRIPLE NET LEASE FROM AKRON'S CHILDREN'S HOSPITAL. WE ARE BUILDING A 23,000 SQ FT OUT PATIENT MEDICAL CENTER IN AMHERST ON RT 2 NEAR OAK POINT ROAD. WE ENJOY GREAT OCCUPANCY AT AVON POINTE AND OAK POINT PROFESSIONAL PARK - SUMMIT I + II. WE ARE IN PROCESS TO REZONE 10 ACRES OF LAND TO C-2 IN AVON TO ATTRACT BOTH RETAIL AND COMMERCIAL DEVELOPMENT OPPORTUNITIES. WE WERE SUCCESSFUL SELLING THE RT 58 CAR WASH AND HAVE THE 20,000 SQ FT WAREHOUSE ON RT 58 UNDER CONTRACT TO SELL TO SKYLIFT FOR A GREAT PRICE. WE EXITED DOCTOPIA VERY SUCCESSFULLY AT 3X AND ENJOYED OTHER INVESTMENT LIQUIDATIONS. OUR PORTFOLIOS ARE ALL DOING EXTREMELY WELL ESPECIALLY OVERCOMING COVID-19. LAST BUT NOT LEAST, JEN CAMPANA JOINED ME AND ANTHONY AT CAMPANA CAPITAL. I AM MOST GRATEFUL FOR JEN'S BRILLIANT GRASP OF OUR BUSINESS. TEAMED UP WITH ANTHONY THE FUTURE IS SO, SO BRIGHT AS ANTHONY CONTINUES TO EXCEED MY VERY HIGH EXPECTATIONS. WE ARE POSITIONED VERY WELL FOR THE FUTURE. WE WILL PROGRESS WITH CONTROLLED OPTIMISM KNOWING THE MARKET CAN CHANGE RAPIDLY ESPECIALLY WITH COVID-19 AND THE DEBT LEVELS OUR GOVERNMENT HAS CREATED. I HUMBLY LOOK BACK ON 2020 AS A VERY SUCCESSFUL YEAR KNOWING MANY ARE FACING HARDSHIP. WE WILL CONTINUE TO ASSIST WHERE AND WHEN WE CAN.

WITH GRATITUDE + LOVE,
BOB

P.C. CAMPANA, INC.
1374 EAST 28th STREET
LORAIN, OHIO 44055

BOB CAMPANA'S
MISSION STATEMENT

(440) 246-6500
(800) 321-0151
Fax: (440) 244-2693

12.30.20

PATSIE C. CAMPANA, SR.
FOUNDER

- I AM OBEDIENT TO GOD THE FATHER, SON AND HOLY SPIRIT. I REAP MY GOD GIVEN TALENTS. I GRATEFULLY, HUMBLY, ENTHUSIASTICALLY AND WITH A STRONG SENSE OF DISCIPLINE WELCOME EACH DAY LIVING BY MY PRIORITIZED VALUES OF FAITH, FAMILY, HEALTH, FREEDOM AND INTEGRITY.

- I AM A DEDICATED, LOYAL, LOVING, SUPPORTIVE AND FUN HUSBAND, FATHER, GRANDFATHER (PAPA), PARTNER AND FRIEND. I TAKE AN INTEREST IN THEIR INDIVIDUAL INTERESTS AND WELL BEING. I DEMONSTRATE THAT "I CARE".

- I AM A LIFE-LONG LEARNER AND CONTINUOUS IMPROVER.

- I AM A SERVANT LEADER (SELFLESS), MENTOR, EXAMPLE AND ROLE MODEL FOR OTHERS.

- I LIVE EACH DAY WITH A MINDSET OF **GHEDMCL** = GRATEFUL, HUMBLE, ENTHUSIASTIC, DISCIPLINED, MEEK, COACHABLE AND A GREAT LISTENER.

P.C. CAMPANA, INC.
1374 EAST 28th STREET
LORAIN, OHIO 44055

PRIORITIZED VALUES

(440) 246-6500
(800) 321-0151
Fax: (440) 244-2693

12-29-20

PATSIE C. CAMPANA, SR.
FOUNDER

MY PRIORITIZED VALUES ARE ON THE INSTRUMENT PANEL FOR MY LIFE AND ETERNITY. I NEED TO FOCUS ON MISSION CRITICAL INFORMATION TO ENSURE I ACCOMPLISH MY OBJECTIVES/DREAMS AND GOALS. VERY SIMILAR TO THE INSTRUMENT PANEL IN AN AIR PLANE - FUEL LEVEL, ALTITUDE, OIL PRESSURE, ENGINE TEMPATURE AND DIRECTION. IF ANY MISSION CRITICAL INSTRUMENTS FAIL I CAN CRASH AND BURN OR FAIL MY MISSION. I HAVE OBJECTIVES, DREAMS AND GOALS TO ACCOMPLISH SUCCESSFULLY. THESE ARE MISSION CRITICAL

#1 FAITH
#2 FAMILY   #3 HEALTH
#4 FREEDOM   #5 INTEGRITY

#6 TRAVEL - ALTHOUGH IT IS NOT A MISSION CRITICAL VALUE IT IS A VALUE THAT PROVIDES GREAT JOY TO LORI AND TO ME

P.C. CAMPANA, INC.
1374 EAST 28th STREET
LORAIN, OHIO 44055

Goals 2021

(440) 246-6500
(800) 321-0151
Fax: (440) 244-2693

12.30.20

PATSIE C. CAMPANA., SR.
FOUNDER

#1 FAITH

- HONOR GOD THE FATHER, SON AND HOLY SPIRIT IN ALL I DO, SAY AND THINK
- ACCEPT THE YOKE OF JESUS DAILY TO MAKE MY BURDENS LIGHT
- PRAY DAILY   READ SCRIPTURE DAILY
- ATTEND MASS WEEKLY   ATTEND ALL HOLY DAYS
- EUCHARISTIC MINISTER REGULARLY
- SHARE THE GOOD NEWS OF JESUS REGULARLY
- READ CATHOLIC AND CHRISTIAN BOOKS AND PUBLICATIONS REGULARLY
- SUPPORT CATHOLIC AND CHRISTIAN MISSIONS GENEROUSLY
- BE A BRIGHT LIGHT FOR CHRIST IN OUR DARK WORLD ALWAYS

NOTE: (1) PASTOR DICK WOODWARD (ICM WITH DOUG RUSSEL) AUTHORED MANY WONDERFUL BOOKS AND PAMPHLETS - READ THEM

(2) LORI AND I VISITED FATIMA, LORDES AND THE HOLY LAND IN 2018 IT WAS A WONDERFUL EXPERIENCE. AN OPPORTUNITY FOR ME TO THANK MOTHER MARY IN FATIMA AND LORDES FOR COMFORT DURING MY BATTLE WITH THROAT CANCER. WHILE IN THE HOLY LAND AN OPPORTUNITY TO THANK GOD, JESUS AND THE HOLY SPIRIT FOR SALVATION. WOW, WOW, WOW!

P.C. CAMPANA, INC.
1374 EAST 28th STREET
LORAIN, OHIO 44055

GOALS 2021

(440) 246-6500
(800) 321-0151
Fax: (440) 244-2693

12-30-20

PATSIE C. CAMPANA, SR.
FOUNDER

#2 Family

- I AM A DEDICATED, LOYAL, LOVING, SUPPORTIVE AND FUN HUSBAND, FATHER AND GRANDFATHER (PAPA) — <u>BE THE BEST</u>!
- 75 YEARS OF MARRIAGE HEALTHY AND HAPPY AND JOYFUL
- AN EXAMPLE AND ROLE MODEL TO FUTURE GENERATIONS TO INSTILL VALUES OF FAITH, SERVANT LEADERSHIP, GRATITUDE, HUMILITY, ENTHUSIASM, DISCIPLINE, MEEKNESS AND SELFLESSNESS.

<u>LORI</u> — A WOMAN OF NOBLE CHARACTER (PROVERBS 31) A BLESSING FROM GOD THAT IS PRICELESS

- BE THE BEST HUSBAND/PARTNER DAILY
- SUPPORT HER INTERESTS DAILY
- WORKOUT TOGETHER REGULARLY IN OUR AWESOME GYM
- TRAVEL EXTENSIVELY IN 2021 AND BEYOND
- GROW IN FAITH TOGETHER DAILY SCRIPTURE READINGS/DISCUSSION ATTEND MASS TOGETHER VISIT HOLY SITES COMMUNICATE WITH RELIGIOUS PEOPLE
- SHOWER HER WITH LOVE, RESPECT AND APPRECIATION ALWAYS

<u>ANTHONY, JENNIFER, SOPHIA GRACE</u> AND <u>ELLA BOVE</u>

- BE THE BEST FATHER AND PAPA
- SUPPORT THEIR INTERESTS PERSONALLY AND PROFESSIONALLY
  JENNIFER - DALE CARNEGIE

P.C. CAMPANA, INC.
1374 EAST 28th STREET
LORAIN, OHIO 44055

Goals 2021

(440) 246-6500
(800) 321-0151
Fax: (440) 244-2693

PATSIE C. CAMPANA, SR.
FOUNDER

- PLAN EXPERIENCES TO SHARE TOGETHER
- ENJOY 30006 LAKE ROAD TOGETHER
- EXPAND ACCESS TO CAPITAL
- CONTINUE TO FINE TUNE STRATEGIC DIRECTION OF CAMPANA CAPITAL
  JENNIFER DEEPER UNDERSTANDING OF BUSINESS
- BE ACTIVE WITH THE GIRLS AS THEY GROW. BUILD PERSONAL RELATIONSHIPS WITH THE GIRLS.

LAUREN, SAM, LIVIA CARMEN, DEMI LINCOLN

- BE THE BEST FATHER AND PAPA
- SUPPORT LOLO SOCIAL
- SUPPORT THEIR INTERESTS PERSONALLY AND PROFESSIONALLY
  SAM-DALE CARNEGIE
- PLAN EXPERIENCES TO SHARE TOGETHER
- ENJOY 30006 LAKE ROAD TOGETHER
- EXPAND ACCESS TO CAPITAL
- BE ACTIVE WITH GIRLS AS THEY GROW. BUILD PERSONAL RELATIONSHIPS WITH THE GIRLS.

NICOLE + GREGG

- BE THE BEST FATHER
- SUPPORT COCO CONCEPTS
- SUPPORT THEIR INTERESTS PERSONALLY AND PROFESSIONALLY
  GREGG - DALE CARNEGIE

P.C. CAMPANA, INC.
1374 EAST 28th STREET
LORAIN, OHIO 44055

GOALS 2021

(440) 246-6500
(800) 321-0151
Fax: (440) 244-2693

PATSIE C. CAMPANA., SR.
FOUNDER

- PLAN EXPERIENCES TO SHARE TOGETHER
- ENJOY 30006 LAKE ROAD TOGETHER
- EXPAND ACCESS TO CAPITAL
- LOOK FORWARD TO THEIR FUTURE FAMILY

CAMPANA CAPITAL WAS ESTABLISHED TO PROVIDE MULTIPLE STREAMS OF INCOME THROUGH REAL ESTATE DEVELOPMENT, PRIVATE EQUITY AND VENTURE CAPITAL INVESTMENTS. THE PURPOSE IS TO HAVE INCOME TO SUPPORT FAMILY DREAMS, GOALS AND LIFESTYLES FOR GENERATIONS TO COME. MY DREAM IS FOR FUTURE GENERATIONS TO BE INSPIRED TO CONTROL THEIR OWN DESTINY THROUGH SELF EMPLOYMENT AND INDIVIDUAL ACCOMPLISHMENT. CORPORATE AMERICA CAN'T BE TRUSTED TO HAVE OUR BEST INTERESTS IN MIND.

#3 HEALTH

I HAVE WORKED DILIGENTLY FOR GREAT HEALTH MY ENTIRE ADULT LIFE. I HAVE ENJOYED THE FRUITS OF MY EFFORTS TREMENDOUSLY UNTIL MY 2017 DIAGNOSIS OF HPV POSITIVE THROAT CANCER AND MY 2020 DIAGNOSIS OF NON SMOKING LUNG CANCER. BY THE GRACE OF GOD, ACCESS TO WORLD CLASS HEALTH CARE, MY WIFE LORI AND DR. TED TEKNOS I AM 100% HEALTHY AGAIN. LEE KOURY PLAYED AN ESPECIALLY PROVIDENTIAL ROLE I AM FOREVER GRATEFUL.

P.C. CAMPANA, INC.
1374 EAST 28th STREET
LORAIN, OHIO 44055

GOALS 2021

(440) 246-6500
(800) 321-0151
Fax: (440) 244-2693

PATSIE C. CAMPANA., SR.
FOUNDER

IT TAUGHT ME THAT I NEEDED TO RAISE THE BAR ON DIET AS MY EXERCISE PROGRAM HAS BEEN EXCEPTIONAL. I HAVE COMMITTED TO 100% PLANT BASED WHOLE FOOD DIET (NO OIL) LORI IS NOW A CERTIFIED WELLNESS COACH AND I AM HER 1st CLIENT. THANK GOD FOR MY AWESOME WIFE.

- 30 MINUTES AEROBIC EXERCISE ≥ 5 DAYS PER WEEK
- WORKOUT WITH LORI WHEN POSSIBLE. SHE IS IN THE BEST SHAPE OF HER LIFE AT 62. — WOW !!!
- FOCUS ON FUNCTION, BALANCE, FLEXIBILITY, STRENGTH AND AEROBIC
- SLEEP IS CRITICALLY IMPORTANT FOR RECOVERY
- INFRARED SAUNA 5+ DAYS PER WEEK
- HYDRATION — 80+ OZ PER DAY. WE INSTALLED CULLIGAN WATER FILTRATION IS EACH FAMILY'S HOME — VERY IMPORTANT.
- LIVE TO BE +100 HEALTHY, HAPPY AND JOYFUL

#4 FREEDOM

- I/WE ARE ONLY ONE BAD DECISION AWAY FROM INCARCERATION AND BANKRUPTCY. (PERSONAL AND FINANCIAL FREEDOM — LOST)
- DO NOT BREAK THE LAW
- RESPECT DEBT/GLOBAL FINANCIAL ANALYSIS/DIVERSITY

P.C. CAMPANA, INC.
1374 EAST 28th STREET
LORAIN, OHIO 44055

GOALS 2021

(440) 246-6500
(800) 321-0151
Fax: (440) 244-2693

PATSIE C. CAMPANA, SR.
FOUNDER

- MAINTAIN MULTIPLE STREAMS OF INCOME (NOTHING GUARANTEED)
- "WHO" I/WE WORK WITH, "WHO" I/WE ASSOCIATE WITH IS CRITICAL
- PERSONAL FINANCIAL STATEMENT (PFS) TO BANKS BY 2·15·21
- FREEDOM IS A PRIVILEDGE NOT TO BE TAKEN FOR GRANTED
- RESPECT FREEDOM! CHERISH FREEDOM! PROTECT FREEDOM!

#5 INTEGRITY

- JESUS IS MY JUDGE IN ALL THAT I DO, SAY AND THINK
- LIVE THE "GOLDEN RULE". DO UNTO OTHERS AS YOU WOULD HAVE THEM DO UNTO YOU!
- CONSTANT HONESTY YIELDS INSTANT CREDIBILITY
  GENERAL GEORGE C. MARSHALL / LEO KOURY
- THE "WHO" IN LIFE MATTERS GREATLY. CONTROL YOUR "WHO"
- REPUTATION IS WHAT OTHERS THINK OF YOU. CHARACTER IS WHO YOU ARE
- TRANSPARENCY IS POWERFUL AND LIBERATING.
- LEAD BY EXAMPLE
- THE SPEED OF TRUST - LIFE RUNS SMOOTHLY WHEN YOU ARE TRUSTED

#6 TRAVEL

COVID-19 IS A CHALLENGE BUT WE PLAN TO EXPLORE AND ENJOY.
- FLORIDA FEB, MARCH, SEPTEMBER, NOVEMBER IN 2021
- JULY TRIP OUT WEST WITH CRUISE GROUP
- EUROPE WHEN POSSIBLE, CREDIT ON DANUBE RIVER CRUISE WAITING FOR US TO USE

P.C. CAMPANA, INC.
1374 EAST 28th STREET
LORAIN, OHIO 44055

Goals 2021

(440) 246-6500
(800) 321-0151
Fax: (440) 244-2693

PATSIE C. CAMPANA, SR.
FOUNDER

- BRECKENRIDGE SKI TRIP CANCELLED - RENT OUT 1301 ABCD IN 2021
- ROAD TRIPS WILL HAPPEN IN 2021
- WE LOVE TO TRAVEL. WE WILL ALLOW 2021 TO UNFOLD AS WE OVERCOME THE CARONA VIRUS - COVID-19.

BOB CAMPANA 2021

- BE ON OFFENSE 2021 MOTTO "GET THINGS DONE IN 2021"
- UPDATE "A FATHER'S GUIDE" PRINT 100+ COPIES
- BE INTENTIONAL ABOUT "WHO" IN 2021
- BECOME A GREAT LISTENER IN 2021
- EXPAND STREAMS OF INCOME IN 2021. BUFFALO PACIFIC,
  ACTIVATE METABOLICS, THERMAXX, OTHERS
- STRATEGIC PLAN UPDATE - ALL BUSINESSES "GO FORWARD PLAN"
- BIKE HIKE W/ LORI
- EXPLORE NEW FUND INVESTMENTS GREAT "JOCKEYS" ARE A BLESSING
- CHARITY REVIEW ORGANIZATIONS AND AMOUNTS
- READ + 25 MEANINGFUL BOOKS IN 2021
- WRITE + 100 MEANINGFUL PERSONAL NOTES IN 2021 (HAND WRITTEN & ADDRESSED)
- HAND OUT + 25 10 SECRETS TO SUCCESS
- MENTOR WORTHY PEOPLE WHEN POSSIBLE

I AM BLESSED IN COUNTLESS WAYS AND MY GRATITUDE NEEDS TO SHINE BRIGHTLY. I STAND ON THE SHOULDERS OF MANY WONDERFUL PEOPLE - THANK YOU! I INTEND TO PAY IT FORWARD GENEROUSLY.

WITH LOVE, SINCERITY + JOY

BOB

P.C. CAMPANA, INC.
1374 EAST 28th STREET
LORAIN, OHIO 44055

(440) 246-6500
(800) 321-0151
Fax: (440) 244-2693

PATSIE C. CAMPANA, SR.
FOUNDER

IBD'S 10 SECRETS TO SUCCESS

Investor's Business Daily has spent years analyzing leaders and successful people in all walks of life. Most have 10 traits that, when combined, can turn dreams into reality. Each day, we highlight one.

1. **HOW YOU THINK IS EVERYTHING:** Always be positive. Think success, not failure. Beware of a negative environment.

2. **DECIDE UPON YOUR TRUE DREAMS AND GOALS:** Write down your specific goals and develop a plan to reach them.

3. **TAKE ACTION:** Goals are nothing without action. Don't be afraid to get started. Just do it.

4. **NEVER STOP LEARNING:** Go back to school or read books. Get training and acquire skills.

5. **BE PERSISTENT AND WORK HARD:** Success is a marathon, not a sprint. Never give up.

6. **LEARN TO ANALYZE DETAILS:** Get all the facts, all the input. Learn from your mistakes.

7. **FOCUS YOUR TIME AND MONEY:** Don't let other people or things distract you.

8. **DON'T BE AFRAID TO INNOVATE; BE DIFFERENT:** Following the herd is a sure way to mediocrity.

9. **DEAL AND COMMUNICATE WITH PEOPLE EFFECTIVELY:** No person is an island. Learn to understand and motivate others.

10. **BE HONEST AND DEPENDABLE; TAKE RESPONSIBILITY:** Otherwise, Nos. 1-9 won't matter.

P.C. CAMPANA, INC.
1374 EAST 28th STREET
LORAIN, OHIO 44055

(440) 246-6500
(800) 321-0151
Fax: (440) 244-2893

PATSIE C. CAMPANA, SR.
FOUNDER

Personal note I wrote in my hospital room following my 5·21·20 lung surgery. I never expected to wake up w/o ½ of my left lung removed. It truly saved my life - Thank God!

5·22·20
U.H.

Go Forward Plan - RMC

I am blessed in countless ways. I will stand on gratitude and walk the talk of the servant leader that I am. My faith, family, health, freedom and integrity will guide my path. My time will be focused on my prioritized values. I will be an example to my family and friends - positive, grateful, joyful, selfless. Lori and I will celebrate 75 years of marriage healthy and joyful. She is the greatest blessing along with salvation. I will continue to honor God, Jesus and the Holy Spirit in a way that our children and future generations will see as the way to →

Salvation and Eternal Life.

My cancer experience (throat → lung) will not define me. God will use my testimony to reach countless people to accept Jesus as Lord and Savior. God has a plan for me and I will do my best to deliver. These lemons will be turned into lemonade. I welcome the opportunity to serve my Lord and Savior Jesus.

I love my wife, children and grandchildren beyond words. I will be an example for them to live a joyful, successful and significant life. Life is not easy but it is a blessing. It is not without challenge so the response is the key. We control very little - one is our attitude - another is our integrity. God bless me, Lori and our family with good health and the fruits of the Holy Spirit.

RMC 9:15 pm 5·27·20

P.C. CAMPANA, INC.
1374 EAST 28th STREET
LORAIN, OHIO 44055

1 of 9

VALUES / GOALS / FUTURE

(440) 246-6500
(800) 321-0151
Fax: (440) 244-2693

PATSIE C. CAMPANA, SR.
FOUNDER

12-13-14
(FINISHED 1-2-15)

<u>GRATITUDE</u> - I AM SO THANKFUL FOR SO MANY THINGS. JESUS OFFERING AND MY ACCEPTING SALVATION. MY FABULOUS WIFE LORI - A WOMAN OF NOBLE CHARACTER (PROVERBS 31). OUR FAMILY - ANTHONY, LAUREN AND NICOLE. MY PARENTS - COULD NOT HAVE HAD BETTER. OUR HEALTH AS A FAMILY. OUR HAPPINESS. OUR FREEDOM. OUR OPPORTUNITIES. MY FRIENDS. MY MENTORS. MY EXPERIENCES. MY CAREER. MY FUTURE. OUR FUTURE (FAMILY) (PARTNERS) (FRIENDS) (BUSINESS). (ETERNITY)

I AM FILLED WITH AND FUELED BY MY GRATITUDE. IT DRIVES ME TO HELP OTHERS. IT DRIVES ME TO BE THE BEST I CAN BE. IT DRIVES ME TO BE AN EXAMPLE FOR OTHERS. I AM COMMITTED TO BE A SERVANT LEADER AND ALWAYS ACT IN A MANNER THAT MAKES MY PARENTS AND FAMILY PROUD. <u>G</u>RATEFUL <u>H</u>UMBLE <u>E</u>NTHUSIASTIC <u>D</u>ISCIPLINED (GHED)

WOW, WHAT A YEAR 2014 WAS !!! FANTASTIC. FLORIDA NUMEROUS TIMES. BRECKENRIDGE IN FEB. NEW ORLEANS IN APRIL. NICOLE'S GRADUATION IN MAY. EUROPE W/ KRYSTYNA + BRYANT. NYC. US OPEN. WIMBLEDON - LONDON GEO. C. MARSHALL MUSEUM. NICOLE'S DALE CARNEGIE GRADUATION. LAUREN - ELLA CAPRI. REFINANCED AVON POINT. SOLD MOM'S HOUSE. SOLD TENNIS CT LOT. OBERLIN PROPERTY SALE APPROVED. DTY CLOSING 12-15-14. NEW WEST LAKE OFFICE - 1290 PCC TO OAK PT. NEW PRODUCTS @ PCC. FFL BRANCH DEAL CLOSING 2014. OCCUPANCY IS HIGH ACROSS THE BOARD. LNB SALE 2014. GOC DEAL CLOSING 2014. TIF SALE OF 1 CLOSED. WEBSTER CONDO SALE. STEREO BC II DEAL $700,000.

1 of

P.C. CAMPANA, INC.
1374 EAST 28TH STREET
LORAIN, OHIO 44055

(440) 246-6500
(800) 321-0151
Fax: (440) 244-2693

PATSIE C. CAMPANA, SR.
FOUNDER

PRIORITIZED VALUES

1. FAITH 2. FAMILY 3. HEALTH 4. FREEDOM 5. INTEGRITY. It took me many hours over many months to reach these Prioritized Values. Obviously they have changed throughout my life but I am very certain these reflect my current position in life.

Peter Thomas helped me to see the vision of my values as my instrument panel of life to help me navigate the stormy weather life offers. Pete alludes to being "Instrument Rated" so you can navigate in the stormy weather of life. I consider my Prioritized Values similar to the Instrument Panel in an airplane. When one of my instruments indicate trouble (Low on gas, Low altitude, high cabin temp., low oil pressure, bad landing gear) I must rectify the issue to be able to navigate. The same is true for my values. I can't function properly unless my valued areas of my life are where I want/need them to be.

- #1 FAITH
- #2 FAMILY
- #3 HEALTH
- #4 FREEDOM
- #5 INTEGRITY

P.C. CAMPANA, INC.
1374 EAST 28th STREET
LORAIN, OHIO 44055

(440) 246-6500
(800) 321-0151
Fax: (440) 244-2693

GOALS

RESULT TOWARD WHICH EFFORT IS DIRECTED

PATSIE C. CAMPANA, SR.
FOUNDER

3 of 9

① I AM NOT BUT HE IS   4 SPIRITUAL SECRETS - DICK WOODWARD (PASTOR)   DOES REGGE (ICM)
#1 FAITH   ② I CAN'T BUT HE CAN / ③ I DON'T WANT TO BUT HE DOES / ④ I DIDN'T BUT HE DID
BECAUSE I AM IN HIM & HE IS IN ME.

- I NEED TO GET CLOSER TO GOD MORE OFTEN. THE "POWER", "GLORY"
  AND "HONOR" ARE HIS NOW AND FOREVER.

  [1 YR BIBLE READ — COMPLETE THE ENTIRE BIBLE ONE DAY AT A TIME - SCHEDULED]

- DAILY PRAYER EVERY MORNING
- A PRAYER OF THANKS BEFORE EVERY MEAL
- BE ACCOUNTABLE TO HIM IN EVERYTHING I DO, SAY AND THINK
- WEEKLY FELLOWSHIP MTGS FRIDAY 7:30 AM
- MORE FAMILY DISCUSSION ABOUT OUR FAITH
- FAST A MINIMUM OF 1 DAY PER MONTH
- SUPPORT CHRISTIAN ORGANIZATIONS - ICM, CATHOLIC CHURCHES
- BECOME A REGULAR DISCIPLE OF JESUS. OFFER JESUS AS "THE ANSWER"
  TO THE "LOST SHEEP" - BE THE LIGHT IN A DARK WORLD.
- SERVANT LEADERSHIP - JESUS AS MY ROLE MODEL
- WEEKLY MASS W/ LORI
- "BETTER TO BE CAUGHT THAN TAUGHT" LIVE THE CHRISTIAN WAY.

DAILY PRAYER:
"LORD, THANK YOU FOR YOUR GRACE - THE MANY BLESSINGS BESTOWED
UPON ME AND MY FAMILY. PLEASE CONTINUE TO BLESS US WITH
GOOD HEALTH, HAPPINESS AND PEACE. MAKE US EVER COGNIZANT
OF THOSE LESS FORTUNATE. PLEASE FORGIVE ME/US FOR WHAT I/WE
HAVE SAID AND NOT SAID, DONE AND NOT DONE, THOUGHT AND NOT
THOUGHT. WE ARE SINNERS IN NEED OF SALVATION."

THANK YOU JESUS FOR THE GIFT OF SALVATION !!!

P.C. CAMPANA, INC.
1374 EAST 28th STREET
LORAIN, OHIO 44055

(440) 246-6500
(800) 321-0151
Fax: (440) 244-2693

PATSIE C. CAMPANA, SR.
FOUNDER

#2 Family

- 75 years of marriage healthy and happy
- Instill values to children and future generations
- Instill humility, gratitude, enthusiasm and discipline
- Instill servant leadership
- Instill Christian faith with the gift of salvation
- Be an example for my family

<u>Lori</u> - Wow, I am blessed with a woman of noble character. Proverbs 31. Far more precious than jewels.

- Be the best husband possible - daily
- Support her interests - daily
- Workout with her 2x per week
- Support Soul to Sole - Annual event + shoe giveaways
- Europe in 2015 w/ Bubby & Laura Bove, Moe & Lina Ruggiero
- Travel extensively in 2015
- Shower her with love and appreciation daily
- Grow in faith together - more discussions about the word.

<u>Anthony</u> - Wow, I am blessed with a wonderful young man. Discipline, kindness, intelligence come to mind when I think of AC.

Cont'd over

P.C. CAMPANA, INC.
1374 EAST 28th STREET
LORAIN, OHIO 44055

(440) 246-6500
(800) 321-0151
Fax: (440) 244-2693

PATSIE C. CAMPANA, SR.
FOUNDER

- CONTINUE TO SUPPORT HIS PROFESSIONAL GROWTH
- PLAN TRAVEL ADVENTURES - SPORTING EVENTS, LAS VEGAS
- EXPAND HIS ACCESS TO CAPITAL
- SUPPORT HIS INTERESTS
- ENJOY 30006 LAKE ROAD REGULARLY - BOATING, KAYAKING, MAN CAVE, DECK, PATIO
- CLOSE +1 SALE/LEASEBACK

LAUREN - WOW, I AM BLESSED WITH WONDERFUL DAUGHTERS. EMPATHY, KINDNESS, INTELLIGENCE, ENERGY COME TO MIND WHEN I THINK OF LAUREN.

- CONTINUE TO SUPPORT HER PROFESSIONAL GROWTH
- 2015 BREAKOUT YEAR FOR ELLA CARRE / LoLo SOCIAL
- SHARE BOOKS + WISDOM
- DEMONSTRATE LOVE AND SUPPORT DAILY
- ENJOY 30006 LAKE ROAD
- CASH IN "FATHER'S DAY COUPONS" BY 6-30-15
- EXPAND HER ACCESS TO CAPITAL
- SHOPPING EXPERIENCE TOGETHER
- MOVIES TOGETHER

CONT'D OVER

NICOLE - WOW, I AM BLESSED WITH WONDERFUL DAUGHTER. AFFABLE, INTELLIGENCE, FUN COME TO MIND WHEN I THINK OF NICOLE.

- SUPPORT HER GROWTH IN N.E OHIO.
- SUPPORT HER PERSONAL AND PROFESSIONAL GROWTH
- SHARE BOOKS AND WISDOM
- SHOPPING EXPERIENCE TOGETHER
- DEMONSTRATE LOVE AND SUPPORT DAILY
- ENJOY 30006 LAKE ROAD
- EXPAND HER ACCESS TO CAPITAL
- MOVIES TOGETHER.

#3 HEALTH

- 30 MINUTES AEROBIC EXERCISE ≥ 5 DAYS PER WEEK
- WORKOUT W/ LORI 2X PER WEEK W/ TRAINER
- FOCUS ON FUNCTION, BALANCE, FLEXIBILITY, STRENGTH, AEROBIC
- DRINK + 80 OZ OF WATER DAILY
- LIVE TO BE 100 YRS OLD HEALTHY - REQUIRES FOCUS, DISCEPLIN, CONSISTANCY
- BE AN EXAMPLE FOR FAMILY + FRIENDS

P.C. CAMPANA, INC.
1374 EAST 28th STREET
LORAIN, OHIO 44055

(440) 246-6500
(800) 321-0151
Fax: (440) 244-2693

PATSIE C. CAMPANA, SR.
FOUNDER

- DIET / DRINKING
    - IMPROVEMENT ON "WHAT" I EAT AND "WHY". FOR HEALTH
    - IMPROVEMENT ON "WHEN" I DRINK AND "HOW MUCH" - TO BE RESPECTED AS A PRIVILEDGE NOT TO BE ABUSED.

#4 FREEDOM — WE ARE ONLY 1 BAD DECISION AWAY FROM LOSING OUR PERSONAL AND/OR FINANCIAL FREEDOM.
- DO NOT BREAK THE LAW !!!
- RESPECT DEBT. GLOBAL ANALYSIS NECESSARY.
- MAINTAIN DIVERSITY
- THE "WHO" IN LIFE AND BUSINESS IS CRITICAL.
- PFS TO BANKS BY 2-15-15.
  (PERSONAL FINANCIAL STATEMENTS)
- FREEDOM IS A PRIVILEDGE NOT TO BE TAKEN FOR GRANTED RESPECT IT! CHERISH IT! PROTECT IT!

#5 INTEGRITY — REPUTATION IS WHAT OTHERS THINK OF YOU. CHARACTER IS WHO YOU REALLY ARE. SPEED OF TRUST - WHEN CHARACTER & COMPETENCY MEET.
- LIVE THE "GOLDEN RULE" - TREAT OTHERS AS YOU WOULD LIKE OTHERS TO TREAT ONESELF.
- LIVE BIBLICAL PRINCIPLES
- LEAD BY EXAMPLE
- IT'S THE "WHO" IN LIFE. DO NOT ALLOW OTHERS TO INFLUENCE MY INTEGRITY THROUGH ASSOCIATION.
- TRANSPARENCY IS POWERFUL.
- JESUS IS MY JUDGE IN ALL THAT I DO.
-

P.C. CAMPANA, INC.
1374 EAST 28th STREET
LORAIN, OHIO 44055

(440) 246-6500
(800) 321-0151
Fax: (440) 244-2693

PATSIE C. CAMPANA, SR.
FOUNDER

- READ +50 BOOKS IN 2015. GIVE AWAY BOOKS OF VALUE OFTEN.
- HAND WRITE +100 NOTES OF APPRECIATION IN 2015
- MENTORS - TOUCH THEM MONTHLY MINIMUM (IN PERSON, PHONE, NOTE)
  - SEEK NEW MENTORS   - BE A MENTOR TO THOSE WORTHY OF MY TIME
- 10 SECRETS TO SUCCESS   GIVE OUT +25 COPIES IN 2015.
  - CONSIDER A "TED TALK" ON THE 10 SECRETS
- COMPLETE 1ˢᵗ DRAFT OF BOOK IN 2015 - "IT IS SIMPLE, JUST NOT EASY"
  "A FATHER'S GUIDE TO A JOYFUL, SUCCESSFUL AND SIGNIFICANT LIFE"

IBD'S 10 SECRETS TO SUCCESS

Investor's Business Daily has spent years analyzing leaders and successful people in all walks of life. Most have 10 traits that, when combined, can turn dreams into reality. Each day, we highlight one.

1. **HOW YOU THINK IS EVERYTHING:** Always be positive. Think success, not failure. Beware of a negative environment.
2. **DECIDE UPON YOUR TRUE DREAMS AND GOALS:** Write down your specific goals and develop a plan to reach them.
3. **TAKE ACTION:** Goals are nothing without action. Don't be afraid to get started. Just do it.
4. **NEVER STOP LEARNING:** Go back to school or read books. Get training and acquire skills.
5. **BE PERSISTENT AND WORK HARD:** Success is a marathon, not a sprint. Never give up.
6. **LEARN TO ANALYZE DETAILS:** Get all the facts, all the input. Learn from your mistakes.
7. **FOCUS YOUR TIME AND MONEY:** Don't let other people or things distract you.
8. **DON'T BE AFRAID TO INNOVATE; BE DIFFERENT:** Following the herd is a sure way to mediocrity.
9. **DEAL AND COMMUNICATE WITH PEOPLE EFFECTIVELY:** No person is an island. Learn to understand and motivate others.
10. **BE HONEST AND DEPENDABLE; TAKE RESPONSIBILITY:** Otherwise, Nos. 1-9 won't matter.

P.C. CAMPANA, INC.
1374 EAST 28th STREET
LORAIN, OHIO 44055

(440) 246-6500
(800) 321-0151
Fax: (440) 244-2693

PATSIE C. CAMPANA, SR.
FOUNDER

TRAVEL 2015

JANUARY — FLORIDA w/ LORI
MEXICO w/ COELHOS, TOMSHACK + JACK

FEBRUARY — 1 WEEK IN BRECKENRIDGE   AWESOME!

MARCH — FLORIDA W/ LORI + KIDS. (PAT JR's HOUSE, SCOTT's HOUSE)
(PATTI + MARK'S HOUSE)

APRIL — LAS VEGAS W/ TRIGILIO + STEPHENSON
— LARRY JR's BACHELOR PARTY KEY WEST 4-30-5-3

MAY — ~~NYC w/ ANTHONY~~ / DAVE + PERRY - SEE MIKE DEPHILIPS

JUNE ⎫
JULY ⎬ OPEN BUT ENJOY LAKE ERIE
AUGUST ⎭

SEPTEMBER — LARRY JR's WEDDING   OCTOBERFEST ZURICH MUNICH GERMAN BERLIN

OCTOBER — ~~EUROPE W/ BONES + RUGGIERO'S~~

NOVEMBER — OSU/MICH. STATE GAME   COLUMBUS w/ LORI TO FIND JEN'S WEDDING DRESS

DECEMBER — FLORIDA W/ LORI
— AL'S 89th BIRTHDAY - TARPON SPRINGS

LORI AND I WILL ADD TO THIS CALENDAR AS I HAVE CHALLENGED HER TO FILL IN THE OPENINGS.

I CAN ONLY SAY — "I AM BLESSED, GRATEFUL AND EXCITED ABOUT LIFE AND THE FUTURE".

RMC 1-2-15

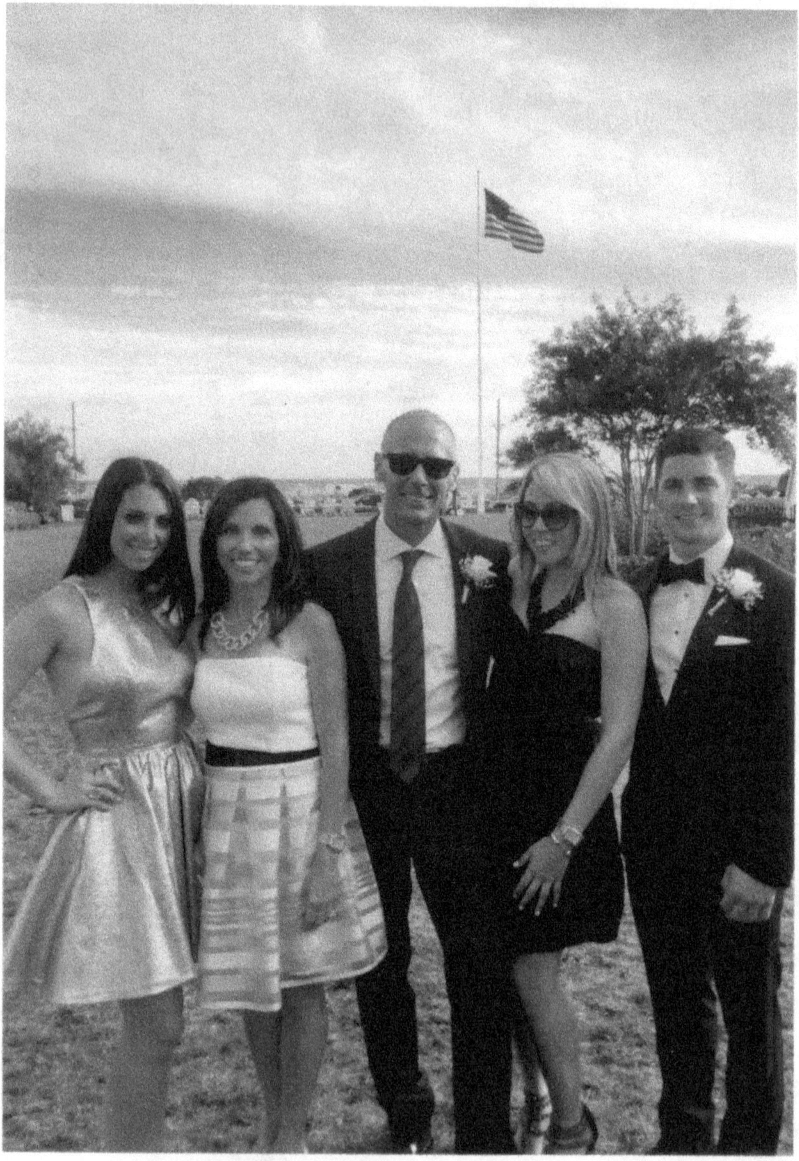